EMMA NAEA ROOKE
1836-1885
Beloved Queen of Hawaii

EMMA NAEA ROOKE
1836-1885
Beloved Queen of Hawaii

Russell E. Benton

Mellen Studies in History
Volume 5

The Edwin Mellen Press
Lewiston/Queenston/Lampeter

Library of Congress Cataloging-in-Publication Data

Benton, Russel E.
Emma Naea Rooke (1836-1885), beloved Queen of Hawaii /
Russell E. Benton.
p. cm
Bibliography: p.
ISBN 0-88946-039-6
1. Emma, Queen, consort of Kamehameha IV, King of the
Hawaiian Islands, 1836-1885.
2. Hawaii--Queens--Bibliography.
3. Hawaii--History-To 1893. I. Title
DU627.17.E45B46 1988
996.9'02'0924—dc19   88-2042
[B]   CIP

© 1988 Russell E. Benton

The Edwin Mellen Press   The Edwin Mellen Press
P.O. Box 450   Box 67
Lewiston, New York   Queenston, Ontario
U.S.A. 14092   CANADA L0S 1L0

Mellen House
Lampeter, Dyfed, Wales
UNITED KINGDOM SA48 7DY

Printed in the United States of America

Emma Naea Rooke
Beloved Queen of Hawaii

PHOTOGRAPHS

PREFACE

Nineteenth century Hawaii produced a number of remarkable and colorful figures. Among the most interesting were a couple of female monarchs. Much has been written already about the last of the native rulers of old Hawaii. Queen Liliuokalani, who was deposed by revolution in 1893. Very little, on the other hand, has emerged on Queen Emma, the consort of King Kamehameha IV (1854-1863), who occupied a central position in mid-19th century Hawaiian history. This small biography is an attempt to shed some light on the life and times of the woman who became one of the island's most beloved persons before her own death in April 1885.

Descendant of Hawaiian royalty herself, Emma was a staunch supporter of the Anglican faith, a crusader for the health and well-being of the Hawaiian people, and a strong opponent of American annexation. Beset by tragedy throughout much of her life, she overcame her adversities to emerge a widely respected woman in a land where women often played only secondary roles. Her attempt to acquire the throne in her own right in 1874 tarnished her reputation only slightly and she survived to be revered by her own people as an elder stateswoman. Accused of being anti-American by her opponents, she was really only culpable of being pro-Hawaiian with a sincere interest in the happiness of the Hawaiian people, a sentiment of which they were very well aware. She was to emerge by the end of her life as Hawaii's beloved Queen Emma.

Queen Emma was one of the major personalities of the old Kingdom of Hawaii, a much revered and loved lady. Her lifetime covered much of the most romantic era in the history of the monarchy. She was the consort of one sovereign, the sister-in-law of another, the mother of the last prince born to a ruling monarch, and a candidate for the throne herself in 1874. Although she came out of that election with a somewhat tarnished reputation, she emerged at the end of her life a much beloved matriarch of the Hawaiian people whose welfare had always been uppermost in her public life.

Emma, the queen consort of Alexander Liholiho, officially King Kamehameha IV of Hawaii (1854-1863), was profoundly pro-British throughout her life. This was only natural considering her background and upbringing and was not in itself anti-Americanism as often thought. The queen was intensely proud of her Hawaiian ancestry and concerned about the welfare of her people. This sentiment was shared by

her husband and most of the native
population despite the presence of a strong
American missionary influence in the
islands in the nineteenth century. In fact,
the missionaries were more than likely
responsible for the royal couple's attitude.
Both the king and his older brother, who
followed him to the throne in 1863 as
Kamehameha V (1866-1872), feared that the
presence of strong American interests would
lead to the overthrow of the native
government, formal annexation to the
United States, and the ultimate extinction of
the Hawaiian race.[1] This fear was equally
strong in Kamehameha IV's consort
Emma realized that Great Britain offered the
greatest checkmate against American
expansion in the Pacific. Being a devout
monarchist, the queen felt that a close
kinship with the British system of
government represented the best interest of
her people and the ruling class of which she
was a member not only by marriage but by
birth.

Kamehameha IV had made his feelings on
the subject perfectly clear since ascending
the throne in 1854. In face, as heir to the
throne, he had opposed an official
annexation movement promoted by his
uncle, Kamehameha III (1825-1854). He

voiced a strong native nationalist reaction to
any formal association with the American
Republic and successfully worked to block
the proposed annexation treaty in early
1854. The fears of the extinction of the
native race constituted the principal
opposition to annexation from among the
Hawaiians themselves, and Kamehameha IV
well represented that popular sentiment to
the proposal.[2]

The king's formal inauguration service,
held at the Kawaiahao Church in Honolulu
on January 11, 1855, gave him the
opportunity to put forth his personal
feelings on the subject in the public arena.
Speaking first in the Hawaiian language,
the new monarch said, "By the death of
Kamehameha III the chain that carried us
back to the ancient days has been broken.
He was the last child of that Great Chief
[Kamehameha I, 1795-1819]. Today we
begin a new era. Let it be one of increased
civilization - one of progress, industry,
temperance, morality, and all those virtues
which mark a nation's progress."[3] Then in
his almost perfect English, with his eyes
directed toward the foreigners in the
assemblage, he said, "Kamehameha III, now
no more, was pre-eminently the friend of the
foreigners and I am happy in knowing that

he enjoyed your confidence and affection...
To be kind and generous to the foreigner is
no new thing in the history of our race. It is
an inheritance transmitted to us from our
forefathers. I cannot fail to heed the
example of my ancestors. I therefore, say to
the foreigner that he is welcome to our
shores - welcome as long as he comes with
the laudable motive of promoting his own
interests and at the same time respecting
those of his neighbors. But if he comes here
with no more exalted motive than that of
building up his own interests at the expense
of the native - to seek our confidence only to
betray it - with no higher ambition than
that of overthrowing our government and
introducing anarchy, confusion, and
bloodshed then - then, I repeat, he is most
unwelcome!"[4]

Emma, although not yet his wife at this
point, shared the new monarch's sentiments
entirely. Kamehameha IV's anti-
Americanism and pro-British sympathies
were very much a reflection of his own
background and upbringing, and were
dramatized by two events during his reign.
The first was his marriage on June 18, 1856
to Emma Naea Rooke, while the second was
the establishment of the Anglican faith in
his kingdom during the 1860's. The king

and his chief minister, Robert C. Wyllie, a Scotsman, believed that if the Church of England was at work in Hawaii it would counteract, to a considerable degree, the American influences introduced by the missionaries who were, for the most part, loyal Americans and Republicans at heart.[5]

Emma Naea Rooke, born in Hawaii on January 1, 1836, was the daughter of Fanny Kehela Young and the high chief, George Naea. She was the great-granddaughter of Keliimaikai, a younger brother of the Great Kamehameha I, thus a member of the ruling family. Her grandmother had married an Englishman named, John Young, who became a trusted advisor to Kamehameha I. Young was once a sailor on an American ship, the *Eleanora*, but in 1790 he settled in Honolulu where he eventually became a royal counselor and ultimately the governor of the island of Hawaii. He impressed the Great Kamehameha with both his wisdom and his honest.

As a very young child, Emma was adopted by her mother's childless sister, Grace Young and her husband Dr. T.C.B. Rooke, a British-born physician originally from Hertfordshire, England. Dr. Rooke (1806-1858) had been a resident in Honolulu since 1829 and had been appointed by

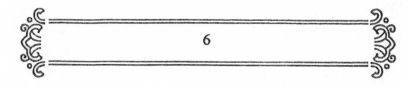

Kamehameha III to serve as a Royal
Commissioner of Public Health in 1853
during a smallpox epidemic.[6] Dr. Rooke
has been described as a "man of rare
cultivation and refinement; much trusted by
the kings and chiefs, whose confidential
advisor he was; and highly educated."[7]
Emma grew up in a refined and cultural
home where Dr. Rooke seemed to have
exercised more influence over her
upbringing and education than his wife.
Little is known of Grace Rooke's impact on
the young lady.

Emma received an excellent education,
one befitting her rank in society, first at the
Chief's Childrens' School, and later from a
private governess. She was most interested
in the heritage of the Hawaiian people, and
engaged in an intense study of their history
and customs, which culminated in an essay
on Kamehameha the Great.[8]

Emma began her schooling at the age of six
when she enrolled in the special school for
Hawaiian nobility where she was one of
fifteen offspring of the chiefs of old Hawaii.
The school had been founded and was
conducted by two rather spartan American
missionaries, Amos S. Cook and his wife,
Juliette. It was actually a boarding school
with the students being allowed to return

home during the vacations and occasionally on Sunday during the term.[9]

Among Emma's schoolmates were Alexander Liholiho (afterwards her husband, Kamehameha IV), and his two brothers Lot (later King Kamehameha V) and Moses, as well as their sister, Victoria. Others included William Lunalilo (King of Hawaii, 1873-1874), Bernice Pauahi, who later married the American banker, Charles R. Bishop, and the last two monarchs of the Hawaiian kingdom, David Kalakaua (1874-1891) and his sister, Lydia, after 1877 known as Liliuokalani (1891-1893). Every Sunday the royal children were marched off to church in a procession, where they occupied seats in the immediate vicinity of the king's pew. Emma usually walked in the procession with William Lunalilo, immediately behind young Alexander Liholiho.[10] Although forced to attend the missionary church services as a child, she grew up to become a devout adherent of the Anglican faith under the guidance of Dr. Rooke.

Since the Rookes had no other children, Emma grew up alone, yet with plenty of love and care. She was said to be an excellent pianist and to possess a good voice, which was low and melodious. She was

equally adept at needlework and gardening.
She loved reading, and after her marriage,
her library at the palace contained the best
of English literature and most of the world's
classics. "Our happiest hours," she once said
of her literary interests, were "spent reading
aloud to each other."[11]

Tall, goodlooking and unusually slender
for a Hawaiian, Alexander Liholiho came
from the same royal background as his
consort. He was a direct descendant of the
Great Kamehameha. His father, Mataio
Kekuanaoa, the Governor of Oahu
under Kamehameha III, while his mother
was the Princess Kinau, the former *kuhina
nui* (prime minister), a daughter of
Kamehameha I's third wife, Kaheiheimalie.
She was the half-sister of the king
Kamehameha III, as well as the sister-in-law
of Kamehameha II (1819-1824). Young
Alexander had been adopted by his uncle as
his heir on October 7, 1853, and like the
other younger members of his family, had
been educated at the Chief's Childrens'
School in Honolulu. He was subjected to
frequent asthma attacks which caused him
much suffering and often interrupted his
work. To strengthen his physical stamina,
it was suggested, at one point, he take up
boxing, a sport in which he did take some

King Kamehameha IV

lessons. Like some of his race, Alexander
was prone to be passionate, and sometimes
quick-tempered.[12] He, on occasions, had
outbursts of jealousy, one of which would
later produce one of the two great tragedies
of his life.

In 1849, at the age of fifteen, Alexander
and his older brother Lot, made an extensive
trip abroad, which took them to both
Europe and the United States. They were
part of the Hawaiian mission headed by Dr.
Gerrit P. Judd, a strict puritan, to negotiate
a more liberal treaty of friendship with the
Imperial France of Napolian III.

The nations had long been at odds with
each other over such things as French naval
activities in the Pacific, and the importation
of French spirits in Hawaii.

Although the mission was not a diplomatic
success, it did provide the future monarchs
with their first look at the world beyond the
shores of the Polynesian kingdom. Both of
the young men kept journals of their travels.
Alexander's had been often used as a
reference source by scholars studying his
reign. In France, they met the Emperor
himself at a soiree, and across the channel in
England, they had the opportunity to talk
with both Prince Albert and the foreign
secretary, Lord Palmerston. The trip proved

Prince Lot, Dr. Gerrit P. Judd, Prince Alexander

most educational and enjoyable for them, and they especially seemed to delight in late night card games and drinking, much to Dr. Judd's disapproval. The only negative aspect of the journey occurred in the United States in 1850, reinforcing Alexander's opinion of America as an insensitive place. While in a railroad car on his way from New York to Washington, D.C., the young prince was, due to his dark skin, mistaken for a Negro and asked by the conductor to leave his compartment. The incident although cleared up before the train reached its destination, made a bitter impression upon the young man and might have been a contributing factor in his anti-Americanism.[13]

Upon becoming king on December 15, 1854, Alexander chose to call himself Kamehameha IV. He retained most of his uncle's cabinet, reappointing Wyllie as Minister of Foreign Affairs, a post which was combined with the largely ceremonial one of Minister of War. Wyllie, who had been born in Scotland in October 1798, had lived in the kingdom since 1844. After becoming a citizen, he joined the government and as a member of the cabinet had worked constantly to stem the tide of Republicanism begun by the American

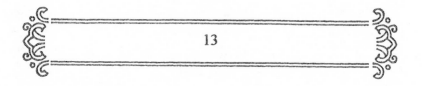

missionaries. He was without doubt the most devoted defender of Kamehameha IV's throne and a man in whom the new monarch had absolute trust.[14]

It is interesting to note that several positions in Kamehameha IV's government were held by Americans. Justice William Lee, who had lived in Hawaii for a decade, was made Chancellor of the Kingdom, and the Reverend Richard Armstrong, a missionary, was asked to remain as the head of the Department of Public Instruction. Finally, there was the appointment of a young American named Henry Neilson from New York to be the king's personal secretary and aide-de-camp with the rank of major. This appointment brought Neilson into daily contact with the monarch, for as the new major wrote home to his family, with it "goes the privilege of living at the Palace."[15] The question of the king's marriage may have concerned some of his advisors, but it was one that the young ruler himself never had any doubts about. Since childhood, he had known that one day he would wed the lovely Emma Rooke. Legend has it that this union was determined in 1836 at the time of Emma's birth.[16] From their school days together, their affection for each other grew into a deep love. Emma added strength to the king's character. She was a calming influence upon his emotions, a "woman of kind and lovable nature who brought to the palace a high degree of refinement and culture."[17] At a Privy Council meeting in May 1856, the king announced his intentions of marrying the woman of his choice, mentioning only her English ancestry, but not the Hawaiian one from which her royal status came.[18] He let it be known that he would marry her the following month, thus assuring the succession of his dynasty through any children born of the union. Wyllie had been encouraging his monarch in this effort ever since his arrival on the throne. Emma was not the unanimous choice of some, however, especially the old chiefly families of the kingdom. A number of them felt that the king should consider the high chiefess Liliuokalani was his consort, a suggestion the romantic young ruler found totally unacceptable. The majority of his subjects greeted the news of the forthcoming marriage with great joy.

The wedding took place amid great splendor on June 19, 1856 at the Kawaiahao Church, the stately edifice across the street from the palace which had been built by the

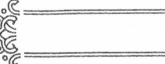

American missionaries. Since Emma's
natural father, George Naea, had died in
October 1854, she was given in marriage by
her adopted father, Dr. Rooke. She was
attended by several of her former classmates
from the Chiefs' Childrens' School,
including Princess Victoria (her new sister-
in-law), the high chiefess Liliuokalani, and
a close personal friend, Mary Pitman. The
king's suite was equally impressive,
consisting of his brother, Prince Lot,
William Lunalilo and David Kalakaua. All
three future kings of Hawaii.[19]

Kamehameha IV and his new wife moved
into the old Iolani Palace in downtown
Honolulu, which had been built in 1844 by
Kekuanaoa for his daughter, Victoria
Kamamalu. It was a large, one-story coral
building encircled with wide *lanais* and
topped by a fancy cupola. It was situated
within spacious grounds enclosed by a low
stone wall through which four entrances
gave access to the estate.

Within the grounds the king had a much
smaller private residence known as
"Hoihoikea," or Independence, which he
preferred as his regular home, reserving the
palace itself for state occasions. Emma was
able to furnish her new home in part with
some lovely wedding gifts, including a set of

Queen Emma in a riding habit

Copeland china and pieces of Pellet and Green cut glass from Queen Victoria, and a complete silver service from Napoleon III of France. The French ruler sent additional gifts in 1858, including a pair of silver candelabra, a magnificent clock, and several hundred pieces of fine china.[20]

Although Emma enjoyed the palace with its rich furnishings and exquisite style, the residence she loved best was her summer home known as Hanaiakamalama, located in the Nuuanu Valley just outside the city. Here, surrounded by the fresh air of the valley, she was to spend some of her happiest days. The house located on the property was a large, one-story structure with six rooms and a wide front *lanai* with six Doric columns. The kitchen was contained in a separate building to prevent fire from spreading to the main residence in the event of a cooking accident, and there was a separate bath house as well. In 1850, the original owner of the house decided to sell it, and it was acquired by Emma's uncle, John Young II, who paid $6,000 for the property. It was he who gave the palace its name, Hanaiakamalama, meaning "foster child of the god Kalama," because he felt that Kalama was one of the native gods who especially watched over the Young family.

When John Young died in 1857, he
bequeathed the place to his niece, Emma.
The royal family frequently used the retreat,
especially during periods of unseasonable
warm weather. The cool valley breezes
helped both the king and Emma's natural
mother, Fanny Young Naea, who suffered
from asthma. Kamehameha IV himself had
a smaller residence just across the road
which was used by his staff during those
periods when Hanaiakamalama became the
summer place.[21]

Emma's husband was an acting monarch
during the early years of their marriage,
frequently visiting various parts of his
kingdom. Emma almost always
accompanied him on these travels. Just six
weeks after their wedding, the young couple
set sail on an extensive tour of the six major
islands which comprised the Kingdom of
Hawaii, giving the people the opportunity
to see how happy their sovereigns were with
their wedded life. On August 9, 1856, with
an entourage of some two hundred, their
Majesties arrived on Kauai, the oldest island
in the Hawaiian chain. From the lovely
valley island of Kauai, they made a brief
stop at the small island of Niihau, then
proceeded to a tumultuous welcome on the
big island of Hawaii, where Princes Ruth

Keelikolani served as governor. They were
her guests there for some time before
heading to Maui and a visit to the old
capital city of Lahaina. Then it was off to
little Lanai, and finally to Molokai before
returning to Honolulu in early November.
Their three month sojourn among their
people proved most successful and endeared
them to the native population.[22]

Maui was to remain one of their favorite
retreats from the hustle and bustle of the
social scene on Oahu, and it was to be the
location of one of the major tragedies of
Kamehameha IV's reign. The impact it had
on Emma was incalculable but no doubt
affected her almost as much.

Henry A. Neilson, whom the king had
appointed his personal secretary upon
coming to the throne in 1854, was an
American who came from a well-known
New York family. He was the nephew of
Edward H. Harriman, the railroad magnate,
and was related by marriage to the
Honorable Hamilton Fish, the Secretary of
State under President U.S. Grant.[23] Until
this point, the king had regarded Neilson as
a totally loyal and trustworthy servant.
However, by the time the royal party arrived
in Lahaina in August 1859, the king had
heard some disturbing rumors to the effect

that his secretary had taken personal liberties with the queen's affections. This was actually malicious gossip with no basis in fact, but it disturbed the emotional monarch considerably. Upset over the possible validity of the rumors, the king decided in his own mind that he had to avenge his wife's honor. On the night of September 11th, he sought out his secretary, and without saying a word shot him in the chest at close range. The shots did not prove immediately fatal and Neilson would linger on for several more years.[24]

No account of the in incident appeared in the kingdom's newspapers at the time although there were veiled allusions to it. Neither Kamehameha IV nor his victim revealed the actual cause of the confrontation. Once he realized that there was no truth to the idle gossip which had linked his wife to the wounded man, the king, overcome with remorse, did everything in his power to make amends for his irresponsible fit of jealousy. The monarch's first thought was of abdication to remove the stigma of dishonor he had cast over the throne. He was dissuaded in this course of action by Wyllie and his other advisors for it would produce what they regarded as the "most injurious consequences" for the kingdom, and play into the hands of the foreign elements who desire to destroy the monarchy. The Privy Council voted instead to pay the victim $5,000 and to take care of all medical expenses as long as they were required.[25]

Emma remained relatively calm throughout the ordeal in keeping with her character. Her so-called "British reserve" served her well at this point. Both she and the king remained concerned for Neilson for the remainder of his life. Their correspondence in the State Archives in Honolulu showed that the injured man was never far from their thoughts.

In October 1859, Kamehameha IV wrote the man a long personal letter expressing his most profound regrets over the incident. He received, in return, a letter from the secretary, accepting the king's heartfelt apology and invited his royal master for a visit. It was the first of many Kamehameha IV was to make to his aide's side over the years in which Neilson lived. In a letter dated November 11, 1859, the king wrote to Emma, "I must tell you that Neilson is in a very critical state. If worse comes to worse, I should like to be with him at his end."[26]

Worse did not come to worse and in March 1860, the attending physician

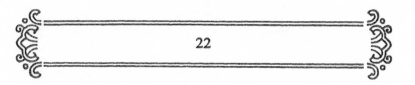
thought it was safe to move Neilson to the capital city from Maui. Kamehameha IV himself made all the necessary arrangements for the transfer and placed his beach house at Waikiki at Neilson's disposal.[27]

In a letter, now in the Archives, dated February 4, 1862, just a week before the aide's death, Emma wrote to her husband who was away from the capital on business, "I hear from John the groom that Neilson is very low, and it is thought not able to live through the week."[28] On the 11th of February, the king's personal secretary died of the wounds he had sustained in the September 1859 incident. Kamehameha IV had visited with him only the day before and found him in relatively good health. It came as a tremendous blow to the king when he was informed of the sad news. This plunged him back into a period of deep remorse from which he never fully recovered. He turned to religion for solace, not that of his youth, but rather the faith of his queen, that of the Church of England.[29]

The king was joined in his quest for the establishment of the Anglican faith in Hawaii by his two most trusted confidants, Emma and Wyllie. Both had developed a deep abiding respect for religion over the years, with Wyllie's coming about as a result

Queen Emma at Iolani Palace

of a serious attack of the fever in late May
1859, which endured for several months.
During that period the foreign minister
became partially paralyzed in his right leg
and feared that death was imminent. He
even considered embracing the Roman
Catholic religion and making a final
confession to a Bishop friend. Prayer
became an everyday ritual for him.

Eventually his leg improved and in early
January, 1860, he was able to return to his
residence at "Rosebank" in the Nuuanu
Valley where he was frequently visited by
the king and queen. Wyllie emerged from
his painful ordeal with a renewed spirit and
a keen interest in religion. He threw his
complete support behind the king's efforts
to establish the Church of England in the
Hawaiian Islands.[30]

There was never any doubt in Queen
Emma's mind about the need for an
Episcopal Church in the kingdom. She had
been an ardent believer in that faith since
her youth. She and the king both felt that
the rich traditions of that institution would
strengthen the Hawaiian monarchy.

The concept of an Anglican Church in
Hawaii was sponsored entirely by their
Majesties personally and not in any official
sense by the Hawaiian government. The

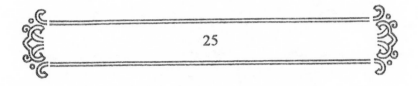

constitution of the kingdom granted all
faiths an equal opportunity to worship.
The Episcopalianism promoted by the royal
couple was not to be established, therefore,
as a state religion, and no government
revenues were used in the creation of the
new church. Kamehameha IV and Emma,
like other citizens of the kingdom, had the
same constitutional rights to choose their
religious beliefs and to support their church
from their own private resources. To this
end, the king offered to give a suitable tract
of land in the capital, and to supply $1,000 a
year in salary for an Anglican clergyman.[31]

Kamehameha IV, in his desire to promote
his newly found cause, wrote a personal
letter to England's Queen Victoria soliciting
her help in the project. Wyllie, acting in a
private capacity as a citizen of the kingdom,
on November 24, 1860, addressed a similar
appeal to the Archbishop of Canterbury, in
which he said that "the establishment of
Episcopacy in this kingdom, *after the form
of* and in connection with the Episcopal
Church of England" was highly desired.
Wyllie's letter seemed to call for the creation
of a complete church organization in
Hawaii headed by a resident Bishop, and
since he was the chief minister in the
government, it implied official sanction.

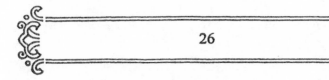
Yet Wyllie "repeatedly declared that the
Hawaiian Government never asked that a
Bishop should be sent out."[32]

Actually, much of the credit for the first
Anglican Mission in Hawaii should go to
an American Bishop, the Right Reverend
Ingraham Kip of California. Reflecting on
the initial efforts to create the mission in a
letter which he wrote in September 1866,
Bishop Kip said: "Previous to 1860, I had
received repeated applications from the
Islands to send a clergyman. The late
Honorable R. C. Wyllie, Minister of Foreign
Affairs, several times wrote to me on the
subject. Unfortunately, we had no
clergymen to spare. In the summer of 1860,
I went to England. Hopeless of obtaining
any clergy from our own country, I agreed
to further that object in England.
Accordingly, when in London in July, 1860,
I brought the matter before the Bishops of
Oxford and London, both of whom entered
heartily into it."[33]

There was some concern in England that
the creation of an Episcopal Church in the
Hawaiian kingdom might be taken by the
American government and others as an
effort to extend British influence in the
Pacific. The Bishop of London, somewhat
relieved, said to Bishop Kip in July 1860, "I

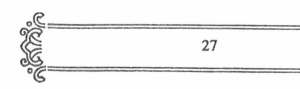

am happy that the application for this mission comes from an American Bishop so that it can not be said that the Church of England is obtruding itself on the Islands."[34]

Emma contributed her part to the project by writing a letter in the most perfect English to Queen Victoria earnestly requesting that Her Britannic Majesty "give all the assistance she could in sending out a Bishop of the Church." Victoria responded with good wishes and encouragement. The combined efforts of Kamehameha IV, Emma, Wyllie, and Bishop Kip produced the desired results. On December 15, 1861, the Reverend Thomas Nettleship Staley, a fellow of Queen's College, Oxford and a tutor of Saint Mark's College, Chelsea, was consecrated as the first Bishop of Honolulu by the Primate of the Church of England, Archbishop Sumner, with the endorsement of the Bishops of London and Oxford as co-consecrators.[35]

Staley was one of three English clergymen dispatched to Hawaii in 1862. Along with the Reverend George Mason, and the Reverend Edmund Ibbotson, he would direct the activities of the new diocese during its first decade. Emma and her husband eagerly awaited the Bishop's arrival in Honolulu for they intended that his first

official act would be the baptism of their
son and heir, the Prince of Hawaii, and
thereafter, the conduct of his education.

Bishop Staley and his staff arrived in
Hawaii in mid-October 1862, having
departed England on August 17 of that year.
On Sunday, October 19th, Staley preached
his inaugural sermon in the presence of
their Majesties, and two days later, Emma
became the first Hawaiian to be baptized
into the new Church with a large group of
the native chiefs and prominent foreigners
viewing the event.[36]

A Charter of Incorporation was drafted
with the name "Reformed Catholic Church"
being used to designate the new institution
within the kingdom. It would subsequently
be changed to the Anglican Church in
Hawaii, but by whatever name it was called
it was a dream come true for Emma and its
other supporters. Kamehameha IV took a
special interest in its activities. When on
November 9, 1862, the morning service was
conducted in the Hawaiian language for the
first time, the king played a major role by
reviewing the sermon beforehand and
listening to the preacher read it over several
times in order to help him with the correct
pronunciation of the Hawaiian words.[37]
Kamehameha IV had, furthermore,

undertaken the translation of the Book of Common Prayer into his native tongue.

The royal couple were confirmed as charter members of the new Church on November 28, 1862, and two days later, Wyllie, along with the Attorney General, C.C. Harris, and other government officials became members of the congregation. The establishment of the Church gave Kamehameha IV a brief new lease on life. The king had attended an Episcopal Church service during his trip to England in 1849 and had reached the decision at that time that the establishment of the Church of England would be more suitable to his kingdom than the cold, spartan Protestantism of New England missionaries. Yet the Hawaiian people, as a whole, never embraced the new faith. Most remained adherents of the religion introduced by the American Board missionaries into Hawaii after the arrival in 1820.[38] Despite the support of the royal family, the Reformed Catholic Church met with stiff resistance to its efforts from both the Hawaiian Evangelical Association (which represented both the Congregational and Presbyterian faiths) and the Roman Catholic Church. The one area in which it made a distinct contribution was in the field of education

Queen Emma with portrait of Albert Edward

where a number of schools were established.
It was for the most part plagued by internal
dissension and monetary problems. Bishop
Staley became increasingly unpopular, and
in May 1870, while he was visiting in his
native England, a petition was circulated
among his Hawaiian congregation seeking
his recall. His downfall was due in large
measure to his "High Church" attitudes
which never were widely accepted by his
native flock in Honolulu. This frequently
led to arguments on points of doctrine and
practice. His successor, Bishop Alfred
Willis, arrived in 1872 and remained for
thirty years, but accomplished little in
expanding the faith. By the end of his
bishopric the Church was still a minor faith
in the Hawaiian Islands.[39]

One of the aspects of the Hawaiian
monarchy which the puritan American
missionaries disliked the most, but which
the Anglican faith accepted, was the frivolity
which seemingly characterized the court.
Both the king and his consort were well
educated and versed in the arts. They loved
the social scene, were fond of entertainment,
and enjoyed the company of distinguished
guests such as artists, actors, and writers.
The missionaries regarded the theater,
whether professional or amateur, as "hale

Diabolo," the house of the Devil. It shocked
them that Kamehameha IV and Emma not
only supported theatrical performances but
sometimes appeared on stage themselves.[40]
The royal couple were equally fond of
dancing which appalled the missionaries
even more.

The one event in Kamehameha IV's reign
which brought him the most satisfaction,
however, was the birth of his son and heir
on May 20, 1858. It was the first royal birth
of a reigning sovereign since the time of
Kamehameha the Great, and sadly the last
child born to a Hawaiian monarch during
the remainder of the kingdom. A twenty-
one gun salute heralded the birth which had
taken place at 6:20 p.m. that Thursday
evening. With the formal approval of the
Privy Council, the little prince was given
the title of His Royal Highness the Prince of
Hawaii, and would later be christened
Albert Edward Kauikeaouli Leiopapa a
Kamehameha. He became a most lovable
child, the idol of the nation, and for his age
was regarded as exceptionally bright.[41] The
young prince accompanied his parents
everywhere their travels took them. In the
fall of 1860, the royal family paid a visit to
Kauai and visited the Hanalei Coffee
Plantation. To honor the presence of the

heir to the throne, the name of Hanalei was changed to that of Princeville. The queen was very fond of sea bathing and during the trip to Kauai, she spent a few days at a small beach on the coast about two miles over the hills from Princeville. While there, in addition to playing in the waters, she engaged in hunting seashells and sometimes the eels which were common among the rocks along the coast. Their Majesties had their own boats and rowing crews with them, and spent a good portion of their time rowing over the waters of Punikaiwa, the beautiful Hanalei river.[42]

The love which Emma and her husband had for their offspring was reflected in all the correspondence between them now found in the State Archives. Somewhere in each letter there was a reference to "baby." On November 14, 1859, in a note Emma sent to Kamehameha IV there was this comment: "Baby is a little feverish this morning. We are all well. Everything goes as usual in this little settlement of the Palace yard." The following day, in another letter, the queen wrote her husband. "Baby had a burning fever on him all night." She continued with the report that her son was "running round the rooms crying and calling for Papa Papa dear which is a new word he learnst [sic] of his own accord for we did not teach it to him." In concluding the letter, she noted "this morning the fever has entirely passed off, the Doctor says it arose from a little disarrangement of the stomach only."[43]

As noted in the correspondence, the child's health was precarious and a constant concern to his parents. In another letter to the king, Emma concluded with "Baby continues little unwell he had a dose of castor oil last night and is looking very sunken in the eyes." By 1861, Emma's letters were more optimistic about her son's health.[44]

In 1862, the little prince was almost four years old. In a letter from Emma to her royal spouse, dated January 19th, she noted that "Baby looks out for you daily, he says put in a kiss for Papa," and in one of May 13, 1862, "Baby is well, with only a slight horseness, [sic]. He asks frequently when Papa is coming home."[45]

The king's concern for his son was equally obvious in his letters to Emma written during his travels throughout the kingdom. In a January 30, 1860 letter, Kamehameha IV wrote, "I am glad to hear that baby appears well in his fireman's costume." This was reference to the heir's honorary membership in the Honolulu Fire

Department and the adorable little red
uniform with the number "4" on it which
had been presented to him on the occasion.
The king concluded the letter with "can
expect us positively by the next steamer.
Send Baby down in the carriage, but with
only two horses." In a letter dated July 2,
1861, the king told Emma of a strange
dream he had experienced concerning his
son. "I dreamt of Baby last night–that he
had succeeded in shifting his clothes, and
nobody knew what he had done with those
he had taken off. Kiss Baby for me."[46]

The king's concern in matters of health
was not limited to his son, but was one
he felt for his Hawaiian people as well. In
this interest he was most earnestly supported
by Queen Emma. The continuing death
rate from disease distressed the royal couple
considerably and led to the establishment of
a major hospital in Honolulu which would
bear the queen's name. Venereal disease was
a major factor contributing to the rapid
decline. It was combined with a long list of
other diseases which afflicted the
Hawaiians. Of a native population of
250,000 in 1800, by mid-century it had
dwindled down to less than 75,000.
Kamehameha IV had petitioned the
Legislature to create a state hospital but

received little from his request. That body
did enact a law establishing a board of
health and furthermore, authorized the
Ministry of the Interior to establish public
hospitals, but failed to provide funds for
their construction. So, on their own the
king and queen promoted the construction
of a hospital to meet the medical needs of
the native population. It was but the first of
a number of social projects carried on by
Emma over the years and was to earn her
widespread respect among both natives and
foreigners alike.[47]

In 1859, the king decided upon a new
approach for acquiring funds for a hospital.
Urged on by Emma, he engaged in the
promotion of public subscription to raise
the necessary money to establish the medical
facility. Setting an example, the royal
couple each pledged $500 and then with
notebooks in hand, they went into the
capital's streets, stores, and homes where
they succeeded in collecting almost $14,000
for the hospital. With this endowment, and
with land provided by the government, the
institution to be officially known as "Hale
Ma'i a Ke Wahine Alii" of The Queen's
Hospital, began service in a temporary
building on Fort Street on August 1, 1859.[48]
It later moved into a permanent residence

and the Legislature enacted a special tax to maintain it. By April 28, 1863, The Queen's Hospital had formulated its basic policy for treating primarily the native population. On that date it "resolved that all indigent, sick and enabled Hawaiian subjects, native or naturalized, are entitled to receive accommodation and treatment at the Queen's Hospital and the number treated would be affected only by the lack of funds."[49]

Emma took a special delight and interest in the new facility. The king, in dedicating it to her on July 17, 1860, had said: "Because of her great heart the Hawaiian people will always have a place to which they can turn in times of need, and this hospital, bearing her name, will stand forever as an imperishable monument to her great love for her people." The queen visited the hospital on a regular basis, setting aside Thursday each week to allow her time to walk through the wards and stop at each bed to bestow a word of cheer and a tender smile. Her presence made the patients feel better, knowing that someone of her rank really cared. When Emma's will was probated in 1885, it disclosed she had left most of her property and fortune of over $600,000 as an endowment for the hospital

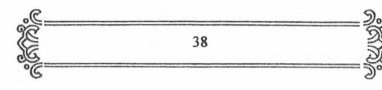

to provide "free treatment for poor
Hawaiians."[50]

Emma had a number of other social
projects to which she gave her time and
interest. Chief among them was the
promotion of education for the young
women of the kingdom. In 1862, the king
had taken a hand in creating a boarding
school for young Hawaiian men originally
known as Saint Alban's Christian School, a
name later changed to Iolani. This inspired
the queen to undertake the same measure for
young women. In 1863, Emma wrote,
"Hawaiian girls equally require a good
education in English, and need to be trained
in nursing the sick and as children's nurses,
to prepare them to be wiser mothers and
wives."[51] The queen's involvement led to
the arrival, in February 1867, of three
nursing sisters from England and the
establishment of Saint Andrew's Priory
School in Honolulu. Sponsored by the
Anglican Mission, the program at Saint
Andrew's placed a great emphasis on
homemaking and other activities designed
to develop the Christian character. Emma
often visited the school for it was her custom
to attend the four o'clock service at the
Anglican Cathedral next door and then take
tea with the Sisters, whom she loved. Emma

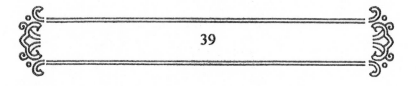

established several scholarships for the school and later increased her support of them.

Emma's interest in leprosy was a most personal one as it involved a close member of her own family, her cousin, Peter Young Kaeo (1836-1880). On his mother's side, Peter was a descendant of the same English sailor, John Young, whom the queen counted among her relatives. As a young man he had contracted what officially was to be called Hansen's Disease and had been shipped to the kingdom's leprosy colony at Kalawao on the island of Molokai. There over the years Emma engaged in a lengthy correspondence with him, showing a most sincere devotion for his welfare and hoped for recovery. She always concluded her letters to him "ever dear Coz." These have now been published under the title, *News From Molokai. Letters Between Peter Kaeo and Queen Emma, 1873-1876.*[52] Emma's personal physician, Dr. George Trousseau, had been instrumental in the establishment of the leper colony on Molokai in 1866.

A tragedy of greater proportions was to befall Emma and her husband in August 1863, the death of their beloved son at the age of four. The event preceding his death has been described by the high chiefess

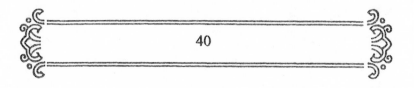

Liliuokalani in her biography in the
following words: "When the child was
about four years old, he became dissatisfied
with a pair of boots, and burst into an
ungovernable fit of passion. His father
sought to cool him off by putting the boy
under an open faucet of cold, running
water. The little one appeared to be
unharmed, but later in the day, broke down
with nervous weeping, and could not be
comforted. Then it was discovered that the
cold douche and shock had brought on an
attack of brain fever."[53]

Albert Edward's parents watched in
anguish as their son's life slipped away.
They remained at his bedside throughout
the ordeal, hoping and praying for the
arrival of the Anglican Bishop, Thomas
Staley, from England, so that the little
prince might be officially baptized if he were
going to die. Queen Victoria had already
agreed to be the Prince of Hawaii's
godmother by proxy and had ordered a large
silver christening cup for the occasion. The
cup arrived in Honolulu along with the
newly appointed British Commissioner and
Mrs. William W.F. Synge on August 22,
1862. It was decided then that the formal
baptism had to take place at once without

the presence of the Bishop, so the Reverend
E.W. Clark of the Kawaiahao Church,
although a Congregational minister, was
called upon to administer the sacrament
according to rites of the Church of
England. Mrs. Synge served as the stand-in
godmother for Queen Victoria at the
ceremony. Four days later, on August 27,
1862, the heir to the throne died. His
passing overwhelmed the royal couple, and
the king never recovered from what he
thought was his part in his son's death.
Whether the cold water incident actually
had anything to do with the ultimate end of
the prince, the king, nevertheless, blamed
himself.[54] Emma, although remaining
outwardly calm, felt that a great part of
herself had taken flight. Her husband began
to call her by the Hawaiian term,
Kaleleokalani, which translates into English
as "the chief has fled" and signed all her
correspondence with that word.[55]

Kamehameha IV was so profoundly
affected by the loss of his heir that he made
no effort to nominate a new one. He did
propose the erection of a new royal burial
site and under his guidance the Royal
Mausoleum in the Nuuanu Valley began to
take shape. It would not be completed until
some two years after his own death. On the

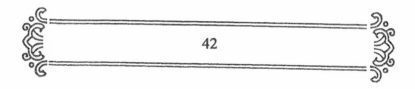

night of October 30, 1854, a torchlight
procession proceeded from the old royal
burial plot within the palace gardens
through the city of Honolulu with eighteen
caskets containing the remains of
Kamehameha IV, his son, and other
members of the Kamehameha dynasty.[56] It
was an awesome sight, and it marked the
twilight of the kings of old Hawaii.

Under Emma's guidance, for her spiritual
resources were as great after the tragic loss of
her son as they had been throughout most of
her life, Kamehameha IV resumed some of
his official duties. He continued the
translation of the Common Prayer Book
into the Hawaiian language and took some
religious instruction from Bishop Staley.
Yet deep down the anguish of his son's
death and the guilt associated with the death
of his private secretary were simply too
much for the relatively young monarch to
bear. He began to retreat into a shell,
becoming moody and ill-tempered. His
physical health, never good due to his
constant asthma attacks, deteriorated
noticeably. At times the asthma became so
bad that he could hardly catch his breath.[57]
Melancholy characterized his entire being
and he looked much older than his twenty-
nine years.

On November 28, 1863, Emma made a
personal appearance on behalf of her ailing
husband at the Independence Day
celebrations which were traditionally held
on that day each year to commemorate the
recognition of Hawaii's independence by
both Great Britain and France back in 1844.
Two days later, which happened to be St.
Andrew's Day within the Anglican faith,
Kamehameha IV had a final asthmatic
seizure shortly before 9 o'clock that
morning. Emma took him in her arms,
pressed her lips to his and sought to breath
renewed life into his expiring body. It was
to no avail. The second of her chiefs had
departed from her. The king died about
9:15, in the presence of the queen, Wyllie,
his attending physician, and various
members of the royal household. The
following day the late king's remains were
placed on view from ten o'clock until three
that afternoon at the royal palace. A large
crowd of both his beloved Hawaiians and
the foreign community paid its respects.[58]
On the very day that he died, the Privy
Council took measures to ascertain whether
Emma was pregnant or not. She replied in
the negative. This left the Council free to
officially endorse Prince Lot, the deceased
monarch's older brother as the new king of

King Kamehameha V

Hawaii, Kamehameha V.[59] For the state
funeral which followed, Emma alone, calm
and beautiful, rode in a crepe-draped
carriage to her second entombment of a
loved one within the last fifteen months.

Emma retreated into widowhood for a
time following her brother-in-law's
accession to the throne in 1863. She retired
to Rooke House in downtown Honolulu.
Her adopted father, Dr. Rooke, had died in
1858 leaving the large frame residence to
her. It was to be her home until her own
death in 1885. The new king seemed
determined to "maintain his kingdom as an
Independent monarchy, in peace with all
nations." Lot, as a prince, had opposed the
Constitution of 1852, which he regarded as
too republican. As king, he refused to swear
an oath to uphold it. In May, 1864 he issued
a call for a constitutional assembly and then
made a tour of his island kingdom to
explain his views to the people. Two
months after his call to convene, the
convention met in Honolulu but spent its
time in useless deliberations which
frustrated the king, so on August 13th, he
dissolved it. He dismissed its delegates and
one week later publicly promulgated a
constitution of his own design which would
remain in effect until the so-called

"Bayonet" Constitution of 1887.[60] In the
new document of August 20, 1864, very little
of the 1852 Constitution survived. The new
Legislature consisted of both elected
representatives and nobles appointed by the
crown. The new document strengthened the
royal power considerably, along with that of
the king's ministers. It did provide for the
Legislature to elect a new monarch if there
was no automatic successor.[61] This
provision would lead to two elections before
the end of the monarchy, for Kamehameha
V was to be the last of his line.

The entire question of succession
remained an unresolved one during
Kamehameha V's reign, for being a bachelor
he never married or produced an heir for the
throne. Legend contended that he definitely
wished to wed his attractive sister-in-law,
Emma, but she preferred widowhood to the
advances of the rather large new king.
Their relationship, however, remained a
most cordial one. She often turned to him
for advice, and they corresponded frequently
on a number of subjects. He placed the
royal palace of Hulihee beside Kailua Bay in
Kona on the island of Hawaii at her
disposal. It had been a favorite retreat
during her married years and she had many
fond memories of her carefree days spent

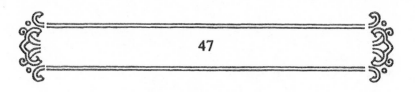

there with her husband and small son.[62]

Kamehameha V's reign lacked the social sophistication of his younger brother's, due in large measure to the absence of a queen consort. Emma remained technically, as queen dowager, the first lady of the land, but due to her bereavement, played little role in the society of the kingdom until after her return from Europe in 1866. Kamehameha V did entertain the noted American writer, Mark Twain, in Honolulu in 1866, whose *Letters From The Sandwich Islands* were a result of that visit. Yet the social highmark of the bachelor king's reign was the visit of the British prince, the Duke of Edinburgh, in 1869. The very fact that he was the son of Queen Victoria lent tremendous credibility to the native monarchy.[63]

Emma decided in 1865 to travel abroad, in part to overcome her grief, but in a large measure to raise funds for one of her favorite causes, the Episcopal Mission in Hawaii. Since the trip took her to Great Britain, it did not escape criticism from some, particularly the Americans living in Hawaii, that it was designed as another attempt to more closely link the kingdom of Hawaii with that of England. The queen dowager's decision to travel was a result of the concern which others shared for her wellbeing. She

had spent weeks of vigil beside the tomb of
her husband and son, often sleeping in the
damp and poorly ventilated vault. Both the
foreign secretary, Wyllie, and the king
worried about her. In March 1864, Wyllie
wrote to an English friend, Lady Franklin,
suggesting that a trip to England might
have a positive affect on their mutual friend,
Emma. Lady Franklin responded on
February 15, 1865 with a personal invitation
to the queen enticing her to visit England
for the sake of soliciting funds for the
Anglican mission. When Victoria, the
British monarch, heard of the proposal, she
seemed to initially discourage it, out of fear
that the poor English climate might
adversely affect the bereaved queen, but
following Kamehameha V's official
approval, the British government virtually
rolled out the red carpet.[64]

On April 30, 1865, Emma wrote to Lady
Franklin, accepting the invitation, and
adding, "my motives in visiting London are
not for display or enjoyment; they are with
your kind assistance and the blessing of God
to save if possible my dying people. From
the great good already done by the
Episcopal Mission, I believe that to support
that mission is one of the best means to save
and render virtuous the Hawaiian people."[65]

Since Kamehameha IV had died on Saint
Andrew's Day, November 30, 1863, the
Episcopal Mission in Hawaii had decided to
make their permanent Cathedral a memorial
to him and to name the structure after Saint
Andrew. This gesture elicited Emma's
utmost interest, and it was to further this
noble cause that she sailed for England. She
departed Honolulu on May 6, 1865.[66]

The queen dowager returned to Honolulu
on October 23, 1866 after an absence of some
seventeen months. As she watched from the
deck of the *Vanderbilt* she saw crowds of
people moving down to Ainahou to
welcome her home. Along with a chorus of
hurrahs, she heard the chanting of ancient
melodies and a grateful people's shouts of
praise at her safe return. She was home to
her beloved Hawaiians.[67]

After her return from Europe, Emma
resumed a more active social life in the
kingdom presided over by her brother-in-
law. She also continued her interest in
religious affairs. She played a somewhat
active role in the selection of a successor to
Bishop Staley when he resigned in 1870.
The Anglican clergy in England gave some
thought to asking the American Episcopal
Church to assume direction of the Hawaiian
Mission at that time, which promoted a

strong rebuttal from Emma. The queen had
been especially fond of Bishop Staley and
his wife, and there are a number of letters in
the State Archives in Honolulu to attest to
this friendship. On one occasion, October
12, 1868, the queen had written the Bishop a
long letter concerning the tremendous
efforts of the Dean of the Cathedral to carry
out his mission and she expressed her
concern about his well being. "Do you
know the Dean I think is doing too much,
not giving himself resting time, and looks
fagged but he won't confess it. One day he
fell down in a swoon outside the little
garden gate of the clergy house."[68]

One of the queen dowager's greatest
pleasures was to be present at the laying of
the cornerstone of Saint Andrew's Cathedral
by Kamehameha V on March 5, 1867. In the
years which followed, Emma remained pre-
occupied with her various charities and her
church work. She frequently entertained
guests at her summer residence of
Hanaiakamalama.[69]

Much of the queen dowager's entertaining
was cut short by the death of her brother-in-
law, Kamehameha V, on December 11, 1872.
Being a bachelor and having failed to win
the hand of Emma as his consort, the king
had designated his younger sister Victoria as

Princess Bernice Pauahi Bishop

his Heir Presumptive upon ascending the
throne in 1863, only to have her die in 1866.
From that point on there had been no
official heir to the throne of the
Kamehamehas. Legend had it that the king
feared naming a new heir because of a
superstition that such a declaration would
hasten his own death. Actually, he had
several choices to consider - all women.
Some urged him to appoint his cousin
Princess Ruth Keelikolani, but she lacked
the western background so important to a
modern Hawaiian monarch. His personal
choice was Bernice Pauahi Bishop, the high
chiefess and last direct descendant of
Kamehameha I and he twice tried to
nominate her only to be rebuffed both times.
She begged him not to think of her but
rather to consider Emma. In a private letter
which Emma addressed to the British
Commissioner, J.H. Wodehouse, on
January 16, 1873, and another one three days
later to Mrs. Wodehouse, the dowager queen
referred to the fact that Kamehameha V had
offered her the crown but that she had
refused it. It was evident at this point in
time that Emma had not given any serious
consideration to mounting the throne of
Hawaii. In fact, she would give her
endorsement to one of her former classmates

from the Chief's Childrens' School, William
Lunalilo, in the forthcoming election.[70]

The queen dowager remained a steadfast
supporter of Lunalilo throughout his brief
reign of little over a year. His health
deteriorated rapidly with the increased
burdens of his new office. Shortly after
being elected, he became seriously ill.
Princess Ruth invited him to take up
residence in the Hulihee Palace on the
island of Hawaii. Emma and a large group
of retainers accompanied him there. The
sea air, the pleasant company, and the
native music seemed to have helped the
king's health improve for a short time. He
stayed there through the Christmas holidays
and did not return to Honolulu until
January 1874.[71] Emma remained concerned
about his wellbeing throughout the entire
time that he occupied the throne. In a letter
to a native friend named Keliimoewai, dated
August 20, 1873, the queen wrote "his chest
pained with the same pain that he had
before." This was a reference to the
tuberculosis which would eventually kill
him. Emma, in the same letter, expressed
great bitterness toward those Americans in
Hawaii who were forcing the ill monarch to
deal with a reciprocity treaty. She wrote,
"the reciprocity treaty, giving away land, is

King Lunalilo

much discussed these days... There is a
feeling of bitterness against these rude
people who dwell on our land and have
high handed ideas of giving away somebody
else's property as if it was theirs." What
concerned Emma and some of the other
members of the royal family like Bernice
Bishop, was the United States' demand for a
naval base at Pearl Harbor. Both royal
ladies were opposed to the so-called Pearl
Harbor plan being promoted by the
Americans in Hawaii.[72]

The monarch's bout with pulmonary
tuberculosis terminated in his death on
February 3, 1874, just a little over a year
after his election to the throne. His legacy
was to be a home for the aged and infirm
Hawaiians which served them from 1881
until 1927. He chose to be buried in
Honolulu outside the Kawaiahao Church,
not in the Royal Mausoleum in the Nuuanu
Valley with his predecessors.[73]

Lunalilo's death brought on a fierce
squabble for the vacant throne between the
high chief Kalakaua and the former queen,
Emma. It was to create considerable
bitterness between the two principals and
their supporters. Although she bore the title
of dowager queen, Emma was actually the

same age as her rival for both had been born
in 1836. Kalakaua, known as "Taffy" to his
friends and followers, had accepted his
earlier defeat with dignity, but now he was
determined to win the throne. He openly
promoted a popular slogan of the day,
"Hawaii for the Hawaiians," and on that
day after Lunalilo's death he officially put
forth his candidacy for the vacant throne.
On February 5, 1874, Emma encouraged by
a number of friends and supporters of her
own, announced her intention of seeking
the throne of the Kamehamehas. In
announcing for the throne she called upon
her "beloved people to assemble peaceably
and orderly in your districts and give formal
expression of your wishes. God protect
Hawaii!" The house was really divided on
this election, for the Hawaiian people had
long admired the queen dowager for her
many acts of kindness on their behalf. She
had widespread support among the citizens
of Oahu, and especially was favored by the
British colony to whom she was bound by
both blood ties and years of affection.
Emma, in her brief campaign, promised that
if elected she would appoint only natives to
office in the government unless there were
positions which they could not fill. Then

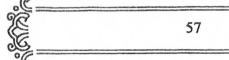

and only then would she appoint a
foreigner.[74]

Mildred Staley, the daughter of the former
Bishop of Honolulu, in an article prepared
for delivery to the Daughters of Hawaii in
1940, said the "Hawaiian people idolize
Queen Emma. They knew - in 1874 - that
she was better fitted to rule by character and
attainments, as well as rank, than was David
Kalakaua." Emma herself felt much the
same way. She seemed to have had no doubt
that she would win the election. In fact, she
tended to take it for granted. Yet, since her
opponent had the endorsement of nearly all
the major island newspapers, and the
American community as well, Emma's
supporters worked hard, distributing
handbills and posting placards, both in
Hawaiian and English, throughout the
capital area which blossomed into a
full scale propaganda war. On one occasion,
a ruckus broke out when one of Kalakaua's
followers added a few words to one of the
queen's posters which translated into
English as "we do not wish to see the
petticoat putting on breeches." Vicious
rumors were spread by both camps.
William Parke, a member of the
government, reported that he had heard that
Emma had promised "if elected to take no

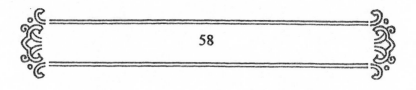

salary, repeal the horse tax, road tax and any other tax they wanted." He added that she had furthermore promised to free all prisoners in the Honolulu jail if she were elected. Most of this was nonsense. Emma's supporters, for their part, spread ugly rumors that the Kalakaua family tree was flawed and largely the creation of paid genealogists. There was certainly considerable wrongdoing on both sides.[75]

With her widespread support among the native population of Oahu, and within the British community, why did Emma ultimately lose the election held on February 12, 1874? Part of it was undoubtedly due to the American interests. Kalakaua had written a letter back in December 1873, which was published in the Honolulu press, to the effect that he had confidence in the good faith of the American government and went on to deny any hostile feelings on the part of the native population toward foreigners.[76] Emma was painted as being strongly anti-American and extremely pro-British by Kalalaua's supporters when it came time for the ballots to be cast. The queen dowager's pro-English attitudes, her open hostility toward a reciprocity treaty, and her outright fear of annexation to the United States all worked against her. These

King Kalakaua

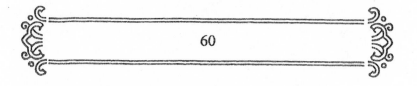

factors, combined with her failure to elicit
support from the other islands of the
kingdom resulted in her defeat. When the
Legislature finally voted, the results were
extremely lopsided with Kalakaua securing
39 of the 45 votes.

It was a serious defeat for the widow of
Kamehameha IV and one her supporters did
not gracefully accept. They took to the
streets of Honolulu, sacking the Court
House, attacking members of the
Legislature, and causing grave concern
among the leaders of the government. The
king-elect, Kalakaua, the foreign minister,
Charles R. Bishop, the governor of
Oahu, John O. Dominis, decided to act
swiftly to restore order by requesting the
American Minister, Henry A. Pierce, and his
British counterpart, to send troops currently
on warships in the harbor to shore. Some
150 United States Marines and 70 British
ones landed that night. The British troops
were dispatched to Queen Emma's residence
in the Nuuanu Valley to disperse the crowd
there. They then returned to occupy the
Iolani Barracks and guard the royal palace
for the next eight days.[77] Hawaii's own
small militia had been disbanded after an
1873 mutiny, leaving the kingdom virtually
defenseless without the foreign intervention.

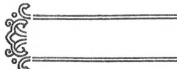

Emma herself was not at her residence
during the disturbances. She had taken
refuge with the sisters of Saint Andrew's
Priory and spent the night in the parlor of
their residence in the company of Sister
Bertha. On the following day, she received
the United States Minister Pierce who urged
her to accept the legality of Kalakaua's
election and to urge her supporters to
refrain from further violence. That
afternoon she publicly implored her
followers to respect the election results and
officially forwarded a note to the new
monarch acknowledging him as the King of
the Hawaiian Islands. Although she had
not acquired the power she sought, Emma
and her supporters remained prominent in
island politics for several more years. In the
February 1876 elections for the Legislature,
the "Emma-ites" as they were known, won
three of the four seats in Honolulu where
they frequently opposed government
policy.[78]

Emma's final years were spent in relative
seclusion, making rare public appearances
and visiting with old friends. In December
1880, the queen dowager spent a week
touring the island of Kauai where she had
once vacationed with her husband and
young son. Never a good writer, something

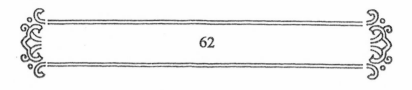
her husband always complained about, she
did not choose to commit her memoirs to
paper. Wyllie, Kamehameha IV's most
trusted advisor, had hoped that at some
point Emma might overcome "her
paralyzing diffidence when confronted with
pen and ink," and put her lifelong memories
down on paper. It was not to be. By 1880,
Emma was generally recognized as an
Hawaiian matriarch, esteemed and admired
by the overwhelming majority of the people.
Only a few of them referred to her as "the
English woman," most regarded her as
thoroughly Hawaiian, almost a national
treasure. She had numerous namesakes
among the young women of the islands, and
the hospital in Honolulu which she had
done too much to promote stood as a
monument to her continued interest in her
native people.[79]

Emma continued her correspondence with
Queen Victoria over the years. Her visits to
Great Britain in 1865 had marked the
beginning of a long friendship which would
continue via the mail for twenty years. In
October 1879, Emma received a gift of a steel
engraving of the British royal family from
Victoria.[80]

In 1883, Emma journeyed to the Hulihee
Palace on the island of Hawaii in the

company of Bernice Pauahi Bishop to attend the illness of Princess Ruth Keelikolani. They arrived shortly before her death. All of the deceased princess' property, according to her will, passed to Bernice Bishop as her nearest living relative. Sadly, Mrs. Bishop did not long survive her cousin's death, for failing health caused her own passing on October 15, 1884.

Ironically, Ruth and Bernice, who died so close to each other, were the last two members of the Kamehameha dynasty which had united and ruled the island kingdom from 1795 until 1872.[81]

Emma's own health was not good during the last few years of her life. In October 1883, she suffered a dizzy spell while at Waikiki, and in August of the following year, while horseback riding at Kohala on Hawaii, the queen dowager had a serious attack of dizziness, sometimes referred to as "lolokaa or rolling brains." The final attack would occur on April 25, 1885 while she was at Rooke House in Honolulu, causing her death at the age of forty-nine. On the day before her death, Emma had complained of a light headache. About one o'clock the following afternoon she had a slight convulsion and a doctor was quickly summoned. He immediately sent for Dr.

George Trousseau, her personal physician, who succeeded in reviving her briefly. This was followed, however, by a second and then the fatal third attack less than an hour after the first one had occurred. Emma had hoped to live long enough to attend church services in the new Saint Andrew's Cathedral but the structure was not finished until Christmas Day, 1886 some twenty months after her death. On the day following her death, her body was placed on view at Rooke House, and from nine that morning until the same hour that evening, a steady stream of people, natives and foreigners alike, filed past her bier to look at the beloved queen. To most she appeared as if she were simply sleeping. Her body was dressed in a white silk gown trimmed with gold. A crucifix lay on her chest.[82]

Emma was given a state funeral befitting a deceased sovereign. The religious ceremony took place at the Kawaiahao Church where as a young lady she had been married almost thirty years earlier. The Anglican Bishop, Alfred Willis, officiated from the Congregational pulpit, using the ritual of his own faith. Then the casket, accompanied by the Honolulu Rifles, and more than two thousand mourners, soldiers and public officials, began a three hour

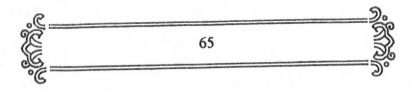
procession along the mile and one half route
from King Street to the Royal Mausoleum in
the green Nuuanu Valley where Emma's
remains were interred alongside the ones of
her husband and son.[83]

Emma left an estate valued at $1,120,361
with provisions that much of it go to her
favorite charities, Saint Andrew's Priory
School and the Queen's Hospital. Her
household furnishings were sold at auction,
with a prized koa bedstead going for $155.
The silver baptismal cup, a gift from Queen
Victoria, was donated to a museum, and the
Rooke House itself was turned over to the
Young Men's Christian Association in 1887.
It would ultimately be demolished in June
1904.[84]

Emma Naea Rooke Kaleleonalani left
more than mere material possessions when
she died in 1885. She left her people a rich
heritage which reflected her sincere interest
in their welfare. Although somewhat
tarnished by the events of 1874, she emerged
at the end of her life a much beloved queen.

Queen Emma

SOURCES

Archives, The State of Hawaii, Honolulu, Hawaii

Daws, Gaven, Shoal of Time; *A History of the Hawaiian Islands* (1968)

Feher, Joseph, Hawaii; *A Pictorial History* (1969)

Hawaii's Iolani Palace and Its Kings and Queens, (1978)

Hays H.R. **The Kingdom of Hawaii** (1964)

Korn, Alfons L. **The Victorian Visitors** (1958)

Korn, Alfons L. and Mary Pukui, eds. **News from Molokai. Letters between Peter Kaeo and Queen Emma, 1873-1876** (1976)

Kuykendall, Ralph S. Hawaii; *A History* (1961)

Kuykendall, Ralph S. **The Hawaiian Kingdom, 1854-1874** (1978)

Liliuokalani, Queen. **Hawaii's Story by Hawaii's Queen** (1977)

Mellen, Kathleen. **The Gods Depart:** *A Saga of the Hawaiian Kingdom, 1832-1873* (1956)

Mrantz, Maxine. **Hawaiian Monarchy.** *The Romantic Years* (1974)

The New York Times, May 9, 1885.

Restarick, Henry B. **Hawaii, 1778-1920 From the Viewpoint of a Bishop** (1924)

Stevens, Sylvester K. **American Expansion in Hawaii, 1842-1898** (1945)

Tate, Merze. **The United States and the Hawaiian Kingdom** (1965) **Treasures of the Hawaiian Kingdom** (1979)

Wisniewski, Richard A. **The Rise and Fall of the Hawaiian Kingdom** (1979)

[47]Daws p. 168

[48]Feher 241: **H.R. Hays** *The Kingdom of Hawaii* (Greenwich, Connecticut: New York Graphic Society, 1964), p. 112

[49]Kuykendall *Hawaiian Kingdom* p. 273-274

[50]From material in the Queen Emma Collection (M-45), Archives of the State of Hawaii, Honolulu

[51]*Ibid*

[52]**Alfons L. Korn and Mary Pukui, eds.**, *News From Molokai. Letters Between Peter Kaeo and Queen Emma 1873-1876* (Honolulu: University Press, 1976).

[53]**Liliuokalani** pp. 19-20

[54]**Wisniewski** p. 54

[55]**Restarick**, p. 273 From material in the Queen Emma Collection (M-45). Archives of the State of Hawaii, Honolulu

[56]*Iolani Palace* p. 5

[57]**Wisniewski** p. 55

[58]**Feher** p. 249

[59]From material in the Archives of the State of Hawaii, Honolulu

[60]**Luliuokalani** p. 21

[61]**Daws** pp. 184-185

[62]*Treasures* p. 16

[63]**Feher** n.p.

[64]**Korn** *The Victorian Visitors* (Honolulu: University of Hawaii Press, 1958), pp. 192-194

[65]*Ibid.*, p. 196

[66]For accounts of Emma's European Trip see **Korn, Restarick**, and **Wisniewski**, as well as material in Archives of the State of Hawaii, Honolulu

[67]From material in the Archives of the State of Hawaii, Honolulu

[68]Letter from Queen Emma to Bishop Staley written 12 October 1868 in Honolulu, now in Archives of State of Hawaii, Honolulu

[69]*Treasures* p. 29

[70]**Kuykendall** *Hawaiian Kingdom* p. 241

[71]*Treasures* p. 16

[72]**Kuykendall** *Hawaiian Kingdom* pp. 259-297

[73]**Mrantz** p. 34

[74]**Mellen** *Island Kingdom Passes* (New York: Hastings House, 1958), p. 16 and material in the Archives of the State of Hawaii, Honolulu

[75]**Daws** pp. 197-198

[76]**Wisniewski** p. 65

[77]**Tate** p. 37

[78]*Ibid.*, p. 51

[79]**Korn** pp. 285-286

[80]From material in the Queen Emma Collection (M-45), Archives of the State of Hawaii, Honolulu

[81]**Wisniewski** p. 79

[82]From material in the Queen Emma Collection (M-45), Archives of the State of Hawaii, Honolulu

[83]**Wisniewski** p. 79

[84]From material in the Queen Emma Collection (M-45), Archives of the State of Hawaii, Honolulu

Book design by Kristin S. Stahlman